THE
BEST THINGS
TO SCREAM INTO

Your Pillow
The Grand Canyon
A Haunted Well
And More!

THE
BEST THINGS
TO SCREAM INTO

ORSON SPOORING

TEN SPEED PRESS
California | New York

It is nice 'n' soft.

2

Crumpled Old Sack

Fill it up with your sadness.

A Megaphone

Scream enhanced!

4

The Hole in a Freshly Toasted Bagel

That is what the hole is for.

The forbidden scream.

6

The Soft Fur of a Stranger's Dog

'Tis a warm, comfortable place.

The Rain

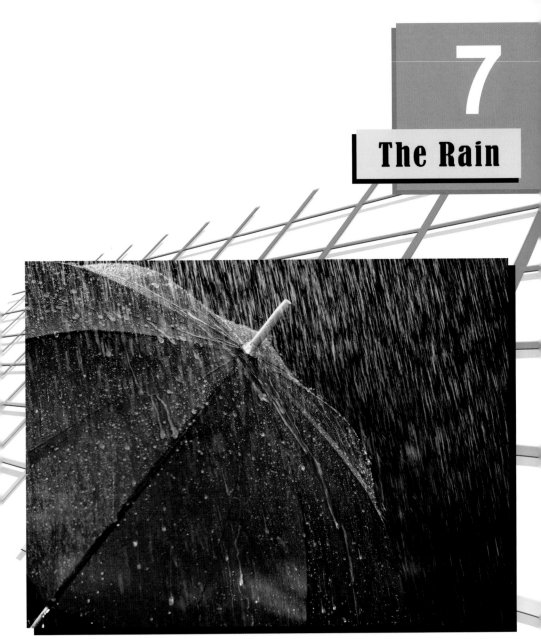

The cleansing power of water.

8

Your Therapist

That is what you pay her for.

A Secluded Cave Deep in the Woods

The ultimate echo chamber.

10

Eddie Vedder's Stupid Face

I don't want you to have to look at him.

He knows what he did.

The Grand Canyon

Nature's most beautiful place to scream.

12

A Warm Bowl of Freshly Made Paella

It makes it taste better.

Science Tubes

A good choice for your smallest screams.

14

Your Ex-Wife's Sweater That Still Smells Like Her

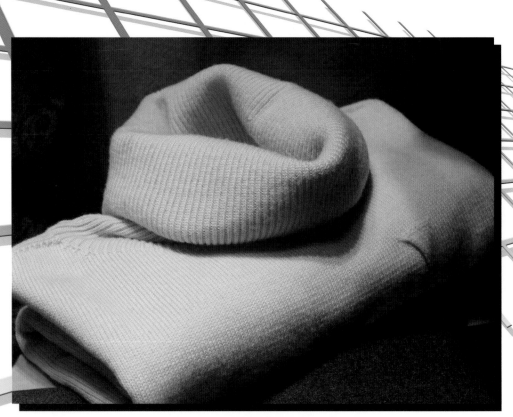

Please come back, Amy.

The Briny Deep
a.k.a. The Ocean

Let the waves wash it away.

16

An Old Boot That You Found in a Dumpster

One man's trash is another's treasure.

Childhood Stuffed Animal

No one knows you better.

18

A Glass Jar So You Can Save Your Screams For Later

Scream storage is important.

The Wind When You Are on a Roller Coaster

WHEEEEEEE!

20

An Alarm Clock

There's nothing like that first scream in the morning.

YOU. ARE. ALL. MORONS.

22

The Office Supply Closet at Your Place of Work

Store your office stress here.

A Hole That You Dug in the Ground

The deeper, the better.

24

New Jersey

Hate it without having to step foot in it.

A Bag of Wet Sand

Superior scream absorption.

26

The Backing Microphone at a Rage Against the Machine Concert

You are part of the band!

Coffin That You Have Been Buried In

I'm not dead yet!

28

A Brick Wall

Get out of my way I am trying to leave.

Your Telephone

That's what you get for calling me.

30

A Glass Elevator

Everyone can see you it looks really cool.

Baby Monitor

Shut up, baby. I am trying to sleep.

32
This Book

33
My Cousin's Wig Shop on 4th and Main

Go ahead. Give it a try!

I do not like my cousin. Please do this.

Go ahead. Give it a try!

My Cousin's Wig Shop on 4th and Main

I do not like my cousin. Please do this.

34

Outer Space

No one can hear you.

A Tornado

Curse its vile destruction.

Abandoned Lighthouse

Perfect ambiance A+ would scream again.

A Saxophone

Music to my fears.

38

A Cassette Tape Recorder

AUTOMATIC SHUT OFF

| STOP/EJECT | RECORD | PLAY | REW/REVIEW | F.F/CUE | PAUSE | TAPE COUNTER |

Listen again and again.

The Bottom of a Swimming Pool

Drowns out any land noises.

40

A Sewer Grate That Leads to the Underground City of Mole People

I KNOW YOU ARE DOWN THERE!

Your Sandwich That You Dropped on the Floor

How dare you I was going to eat that.

42

An Electric Fan

Try it your voice sounds cool.

The Burrow in a Tree Where Some Squirrels Live

Fuck off, squirrels.

A Haunted Well

Maybe the ghosts will join you?

Herd of Zebras

Hahaha . . . stampede!

46

My Friend Randy's Open Mouth

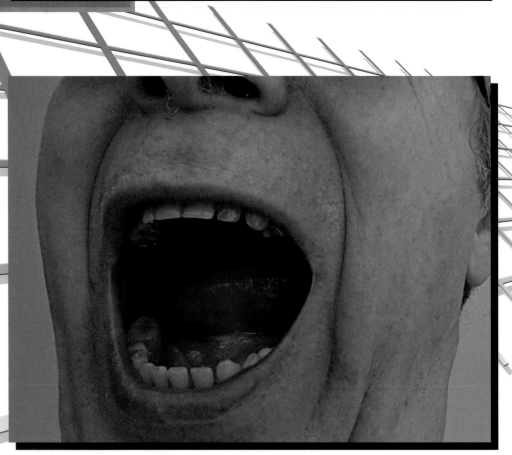

He will let you just ask.

The Freezing Cold

You can see your breath!

48

A Crowded Bus

Several people will already be doing it.

An easy way to double the anger.

50

Empty Wallet

Why is it always empty?

A Waterfall as You Are Falling off of It

Maybe the canoe will break your fall?

Two Cats Fighting
Over a Slice of Ham

Back off, cats! That ham is mine.

A Hollowed-Out Watermelon

The acoustics are amazing.

54

The Lawn Gnome in Your Neighbor's Front Yard

I saw you move . . . ANSWER ME!

A Painting at the Louvre in Paris, France

I traveled 3,000 miles for this.

A Magician's Hat

He will make it disappear.

The #1 gold standard.

Also from Obvious Plant

Animals I Want to Fight

So You Want to be a Wig Model

The Best Things to Cry Into

Erotic Word Searches

Don't Try: A Guide to Giving Up on Your Dreams

How to Smoke Weed Out of Anything

Ugly Babies: A Picture Book

Please Take Me Back, Amy
(I Can Change)

No part of this book may be reproduced, copied, recorded, set on fire, eaten or thrown into a very deep lake without written permission from the publisher. That would be very rude; how dare you.

Originally self-published by the author in slightly different form in 2020.

Library of Congress Control Number: 2020942561

Hardcover ISBN: 978-1-9848-5960-0
eBook ISBN: 978-1-9848-5961-7

Printed in the United States of America

Editor and Designer: Jeff Wysaski
Associate Editor: Katrin Davis
Visual Consultant: Salad Landers

Page 36: Baby monitor photo provided by Jorge Barrios Riquelme and used under Creative Commons.

10 9 8 7 6 5 4 3 2 1

First Ten Speed Press Edition